How to Get Your Ex Back

Strategies For Rekindling A Romantic Relationship With A Former Partner, Geared Towards Men Boxed Set: A Comprehensive Solution For Capturing The Affection Of The Woman You Adore

Royston Alderson

TABLE OF CONTENT

complaining For The Purposes Of Completing 1

Making The Transition To A Stress-Free Reunion Easier 5

The Stage Of Contact 17

Choose If You Actually Want Your Ex Back 33

Getting The Best Ever Happy After Badge 47

An Appropriate Amount Of Organisation And Impact 61

Management Tips For Overcoming A Crush Or Lost Relationship 70

Perservance As A Virtue 93

When A Favorable Relationship Goes Well 116

Entertaining Them Back Into Your Life 128

COMPLAINING FOR THE PURPOSES OF COMPLETING

Women may desire to reconcile with their ex-partners just because they can. They are trying to level the odds or make a statement about their ability to make a man fall on their knees. I will tell you something that will disappoint you if you read this book to support a position.

If your reasons for wanting to restart the relationship aren't sincere, don't even try. If your goal in wanting him back is to prove something to yourself, get him back so you can dump him later, or

Go ahead, others, don't.

In the long run, there is no true sense of fulfillment from this kind of endeavor. When the dust finally settles, it makes you feel a great degree of regret and disappointment in yourself.

This article is intended to assist women who wish to reignite romantic relationships that have the potential to be amazing, life-altering encounters. This guide is not meant to be a trick book for folks who have a grudge.

Relationship restoration is not about making points. The human heart, the most amazing thing in the world, is at work. Respectably.

It's not a game. The majority Approach it with caution and seriousness.

Making up for the insurance industry

The implication of making up for the sake of making up is this. Some women are eager to resume a relationship for the sole purpose of having a guy in their lives.

For many folks, it's more about the sense of security of being in a relationship than the particular connection or the man in question.

If you feel like that about yourself, please reconsider before trying to win back your ex-boyfriend. Reuniting for the sole sake of comfort and insurance is inappropriate, just like making up for the sake of making up.

Men may be annoying, but at the end of the day, they are people too, and like us, they should have their hearts treated with kindness.

In addition, there's a pragmatic reason to avoid reviving old connections just for security's sake. While you're squandering time in a relationship that will never work,

MAKING THE TRANSITION TO A STRESS-FREE REUNION EASIER

This is the best thing you can ever do for yourself in a relationship. By acknowledging your previous errors and embracing the possibility that you will have to make amends in the future, you can make the path straight and easy. Although there is never a simple relationship, we attempt to keep it lively by avoiding the easy mistakes we are prone to make regularly. Make an effort to celebrate with your partner and give yourself permission to be hidden and motivated by the love you shared in the past.

It's time to remember the wonderful times you two had. You can indeed handle a reunion without worry now that you thoroughly understand the common reasons why relationships end.

How to Get Ready for a Smooth Reunion
A seamless, stress-free reunion can be achieved by following a straightforward process. Dealing with a breakup is never easy. It's hard to be composed when you lose someone you love. However, you must maintain your composure. It's a guaranteed method to win your ex back. Some of these are common blunders made by persons attempting to win their ex back. If you want your ex back in your arms, try to avoid the following negative situations as much as possible.

Transform yourself

Recall that getting your ex back is not an easy feat. The situation will only worsen if you start acting strangely and promise yourself that you'll change to get your girlfriend back. Right now, everything you do should be sincere and truthful. Avoid appearing hopeless and unable to regulate your emotions. It doesn't seem like your ex decided to part ways with you based on your traits or characteristics. Should that be the case, they wouldn't have waited until now to end their relationship. You can, however, alter certain aspects of yourself without going too far.

very attentive to other people

This is a typical error made by those attempting to reunite with their former partner. You'll likely receive advice from people everywhere after telling your friends and family. Everyone appears to have an opinion on the subject that they believe to be correct. You need to use caution while selecting advisors. Remember, you know your former partner better than anyone else. This important reminder will, therefore, enable you to quickly sort through all of the positive and negative remarks.

Continue working to get them back.
Are you interested in regaining your ex? You have to do your hardest! This entails carefully considering your options,

planning, and acting! Even when they know deep down that they truly want their ex-partner back, some people purposefully put off thinking about getting them back. They believe they may enjoy a little time together as a single before reuniting as a couple. Consequently, this is a big no-no. Remember that your ex can decide to leave you permanently; extending the time would only allow them to distance themselves from you.

conversing via a third party
After the split, everything you say and do matters. Being outspoken makes it difficult to stay composed. However, saying anything amusing could just lead

to more distance between the two of you. Asking a third party to deliver a message is a common mistake many people make. Give up! Never presume that someone else can do the task for you. Inform your former partner personally. Additionally, when spoken by someone else, the messages may alter, which could result in more errors.

If you take the time to carefully consider each step and create a plan for what you want to achieve in the end, you may avoid many post-breakup problems. Try to regulate your feelings, and proceed with extreme caution when taking advice from others. You don't want to commit any more errors. Thus, exercise greater caution, have faith in your judgment, and steer clear of blunders to ensure a happy reconciliation.

Turn become a constructive force in his life.

Should you wish to win your former partner back, you should start being a constructive role model for him. Although you can't force him to want to spend time with you again, you may take constructive action to win him back. He'll feel better about himself and want to hang out with you more if you positively impact his life. Refrain from acting overly sentimental or dramatizing with your former partner during the no-contact period. Remember to take care of yourself occasionally. Instead, concentrate on your relationship objectives and mental calm. Control your negative feelings and anxieties because they will make the procedure more difficult.

Be a positive role model in his life: If you want your former partner back, improve and strengthen your identity. Develop into a really valuable woman. Smothering your ex is never a good way to get him to want to be with you. You must be upbeat and demonstrate to him your worth as a person. When it comes to love, desperation is a potent turnoff. Conversely, contentment is a magnet, drawing your former partner towards you.

What men desire, they cannot have.

If you're wondering how to win your former partner back, remember that you shouldn't let your feelings dictate your behavior. Men prefer to feel in charge and wanted, so if you come out as desperate, you might end up with someone else. Determine what caused the breakup and make the necessary changes if you want your ex back. Giving your ex some space may seem unproductive, but he'll probably be relieved to see you again.

Gaining your ex-boyfriend back requires being a trustworthy friend and confidante. This entails paying attention to him and honoring his personal space. If you remain a friend and confidant, your ex-boyfriend will understand that you care about him and are happy for his well-being. Similarly, your ex-boyfriend will like to see you in the same light as before. You may quickly win back your ex-boyfriend by using the advice in this article.

Become his pal.

Regaining your ex's friendship is a terrific strategy to win him back.

Although it may seem counterintuitive, this strategy has shown to be quite successful. Men have a propensity to cling to the things they cherish. Aim to evoke pleasant memories. When men learn that their girlfriend has moved on to someone else, they frequently withdraw from the relationship since they can be very loyal to their partners. You might tell him that you appreciate their connection and want to keep developing your bond by being buddies.

Aim to keep the relationship from being forced. It will make him more distant if you try to get back together with your ex quickly after the breakup. Rather, try to enjoy yourselves with each other. Make sure your life is getting better. He will remember the enjoyable times you had together. If you do this, your ex will want to hang out with you again. Keep a positive outlook on the issue as you implement these modifications.

THE STAGE OF CONTACT

In a few months, you might find yourself in this stage of the procedure. Alternatively, it could take a lot longer to arrive here. Just as every relationship is different and takes time to develop, so does every woman trying to get her ex back. Trying to move too quickly before you and your ex are ready to take things further is pointless.

During the final phase of the process, regardless of whether your ex has found someone, you will have:

Get back in touch with your former partner.

Showed him how you've evolved and how easily and self-assured you are in your skin.

Put him in a frame of mind where he feels at ease in social settings and treats you as an acquaintance.

Stayed warm but collected so he wouldn't see you as just a friend, a mother figure, or an aunt who causes him pain.

These are fantastic accomplishments. They make up an essential initial step in getting your ex back permanently. But you could stay in this stage indefinitely if you're not careful. It's crucial to continue with the program when you're both ready.

However, how will I know when to press the issue further?

The following are indicators that you are prepared for the next step: Has he broken up with anybody else? If he met someone else? Is he now back on his own?

Does he feel at ease when you two are the only ones together?

Is remembering the excellent times you had together easy and enjoyable for him?

Watch out for any cues your ex may leave you, but try not to read too much into seemingly innocent circumstances. You've made a new life, and he might be extremely impressed. It could be that he is starting to realize how much he has lost.

If you believe your former partner is trying to get back together, find out if a reliable buddy shares your perspective.

Suppose she responds positively, congrats. Pay attention to the signs to navigate into a new relationship. Go to Chapter Seven for information on solidifying and reinforcing your growing relationship.

Regretfully, not all former partners are as amicable.

Your ex may have discovered he needs you, but he's still too smug or ashamed to tell you. Alternatively, he might require further motivation to recognize the value he possesses in you.

If so, it's time for Activity #5, the informal date.

Perhaps in the earlier phase of the process, you proposed to your ex that you two get together casually. Hopefully, a handful have been approved by your ex. You have had some enjoyable occasions as friends over the past few months, free from the stress of your failing relationship and its negative emotional dynamic.

Now is the perfect moment to schedule a slightly more formal meet-up.

How do you plan the ideal date, sort of?

There must be only the two of you. It should go without saying that this.

It must be scheduled properly. Pay attention to the events in his life and seize the chance. If he has achieved his fitness objectives for the New Year or received a job promotion, this is your chance. Offer to take him out for a "special celebration" as a suggestion.

Avoid using the word "date." You do not wish to frighten him. Give him some room to speculate.

It must have a tiny hint of uniqueness. Make sure this date differs from your typical haunts, but don't go overboard. Suggest a cocktail bar if the pub is where you usually gather. Offer to meet for dinner if you usually have lunch.

Present yourself in a perfectly presentable, but not overly so, old clothes of his. Bring a tiny, heartfelt congrats present that demonstrates how well you know your former partner's preferences. Something that will resonate with him and remind him of your kindness.

There must be an electric mood there. Unaware that he has been talked into a "sort-of" date, your ex should feel this is somehow different from past occasions when you two have met as friends.

Maintaining the right environment will help you reach this equilibrium. Don't even feign a hint of nervousness. Recall that you are easily enchanting, intriguing, and attractive on this date.

Without being clingy, you find what he says fascinating.

You pay attention to the tone of the conversation while maintaining your individuality and beliefs. Move it gently away from anything that could hurt or cause friction.

Once you've settled down, you can start flirting in a classy yet subtle way. Begin modestly. Pay attention to your ex's indications, and if he seems uncomfortable, back off.

Instead of focusing on the past, it must be about the future. This is a crucial matter. If it feels appropriate, you can now discuss more romantic memories you have in common but avoid dwelling on the past and all of the mistakes made. You want to enter into a fresh, new kind of connection. Both of you have transformed.

Speaking your path to success

Avoid posing complicated queries. For example, asking, "Do you still love me?" is inappropriate.

Be truthful without giving everything up. Don't become too serious. Don't express your desire for him to return in great detail. Instead, talk more about your goals, aspirations, and hopes. It all comes down to showing him how attractive you are as a partner—how discerning, wise, skilled, and elegant you are—without making it obvious how hard you are trying.

Even when you feel that way, try not to wax poetic about how much you need and love him. By now, the course should have helped you develop a more impartial viewpoint. Neither you nor your former partner are flawless. You might be in love with him. You may think he's the one. He might be the one for you, but keep in mind these two things:

Like you, your ex is flawed and prone to mistakes.

And you could manage without him if you had to. Although difficult, you could succeed.

As your time together progresses, have these two ideas in mind. You'll discover that they relieve tension and support your continued happiness and relaxation. You're a lovely woman with choices and a self-sufficient life. This date is not the final word. Ultimately, you will find contentment and satisfaction regardless of how things turn out. Your life will function more smoothly, and you will have less anxiety once you acknowledge that.

Finally, don't forget to back off. Don't presume to be an expert on your ex. He, too, will have changed. You can re-acquaint yourself with him and deepen your relationship with him today.

Be respectful and courteous, and keep the same respectful distance you would on a first date.

It's a slow courtship. Once more, you are getting to know one another. You're not reentering a relationship right away. Even though it might not feel like it, you are embarking on a new relationship and starting again.

Additionally, avoid trying to hasten the bonding process. Although it will require some time, your bond will be stronger in the end.

Flaunt oneself in public.

Sapping at your ex in public forums indicates that you haven't moved past them.

The truth is that when we are genuinely free of the stiflingly bad emotions that breakups tend to produce, we have no emotional tie to our ex or the life they may be leading at this point.

It is not necessary to trash-talk or post ambiguous things in this state. You won't care once you've moved on from your ex.

When you recognize your ex

It might be difficult to end a relationship with a known person. This is accurate since you share a connection with all the individuals who came before them who were similar to them.

Even when they are problematic, the connections from our early years serve as a prototype for what we are accustomed to. Furthermore, familiarity may indicate that we ignore or don't know how to interact with different types of individuals, even though they might benefit us.

In a relationship, familiarity and comfort are two distinct things.

Simply put, if something seems familiar to you, it suggests you've probably experienced something similar previously. On the other hand, being at ease with someone means you may be who you are without worrying about the consequences of your thoughts, feelings, or beliefs.

Which would you prefer, comfort or familiarity?

Idealising your ex too much

This may also be a significant factor in most people's feelings of being stuck.

This happens when we refuse to accept someone for who they truly are. And elevate them to a lofty, unattainable, inaccurate pinnacle of greatness.

It resembles having rose-colored glasses on or thinking that things are much better than they are.

When we over-idealize our ex-partner, I mean to say that we stop acknowledging the part they played in the split and instead start pining for someone who never was.

Breakups are difficult, as I have repeatedly stated. A broken heart can have major psychological and emotional repercussions that, in time, might develop into harmful habits that gravely jeopardize your happiness.

The hang-ups above indicate that you're still having trouble moving on after your breakup, positive or negative. The first step towards returning to genuine happiness and fulfillment—and potentially towards meeting someone new to restart your love life—is realizing who is preventing you from moving forward.

You may wonder, "How do I get past them," now that you know what could be causing your hang-ups.

You'll get the answers to that excellent question in the upcoming chapter.

CHOOSE IF YOU ACTUALLY WANT YOUR EX BACK

Of the three important questions posed at the start of this book, which do you still remember asking yourself? Do you still have feelings for your ex? You probably think you can skip this chapter if you answer "yes" to that question. However, rationally, it might not be the case at all.

Relationships are one of the many grey areas in life, but there are still good and terrible reasons to want your ex back.

A Moment To Ponder

Certain connections are destined to endure forever and become stronger over time. But some relationships are better left in the past and forgotten or doomed from the beginning. This chapter will teach you whether your reasons for wanting to reconcile with your ex-partner will work in your favor or against you.

You're Still Attached To Your Ex

This is perhaps the best argument for attempting to get your ex back. The outcome is merely coincidental. For now, the only thing that counts is that you tried your hardest. If everything doesn't work out in the end, at least you won't spend your life worrying about what more you could have done to win your ex back.

You are accountable for the past events that occurred.

Even love and guilt can be strong emotions, using guilt to get your ex back is not a good idea. You just have to learn to live with your guilt until time and forgiveness allow it to disappear if there is no love. Reuniting with an ex-lover out of remorse can only cause further suffering.

You'd Like to Give It Another Go

While that might not be the best argument to get your ex back, it's also not bad. You can still fall in love even though it's likely that none of you or either side fell in love with the other the first time.

If this is why you wish to make amends with your former partner, don't convey any false impressions about your plans. Lying is never a good foundation for a relationship, and it can also merely muddy the waters between you and your ex.

You believe that the Present is your fault.

You didn't end things badly when you broke up. But you started feeling bad when you learned how miserable your ex is. Although that makes sense, it isn't a strong enough justification to get back together with your ex. To find out if what you truly want to offer is an apology, companionship, or a second shot at love, you need to ask additional questions.

You sense isolation

It's undoubtedly one of the worst, if not the worst, justifications for wanting your ex back. Seeking solace from loneliness in your ex's company would be self-serving. You might benefit from reuniting with your ex, but what about them? Do you think it will impact your ex's feelings?

What will happen if the other person finds out why you want to make amends? Is it going to be nice or bad?

You may have several reasons, not all of which may be accurate. Ultimately, you must listen to your heart as much as your logic.

Is it the correct thing to do, and is it something you want back?

Her Inquiries

"Why couldn't you have made these changes years ago?" is one of the things he will remark. Why did you change just after I left? I apologize for the harm that was done. Is this partnership simply too distant? I'm not in love with you, and I don't think I ever will be, even though I adore you as a friend and father.

CURRENTLY BELOW One issue unites ALL of these statements: a decline in confidence. It is essentially vulnerable to feel love for someone. Your wife needs to first trust you before she can fall in love with you once more. Thus, constancy and empathy are the key components of this third step—demonstrating to your wife how you have changed and improved her life.

You need to imagine yourself in your wife's position and figure out what will cause her to pause. Then you need to give it to her consistently. It makes no difference if you speak with your wife every day, once a week, once a month, just over the phone, only through messages, or only when you drop the kids off.

That element is out of your control. No matter how you go about it, your current objective is to always come across as a self-assured, devoted husband to your wife. The important thing is that you take advantage of every chance your wife offers you to influence her emotions. Although you can't make her give you these chances, you can seize them when she does.

Regardless of how this separation turns out, you are doing the best you can if you take full advantage of the things you can control. And that's the main idea behind the 3+1 separation approach.

It's about providing yourself the best chance to salvage your marriage and alter your wife's perception of you within the specific parameters of your situation.

These Techniques Function Like Spells

These are the three actions that I have witnessed countless genuine men take to keep their marriages intact after a breakup. Before closing this chapter, let's review these three steps again. First step: end your desperation and concentrate on the things you can manage. Step 2: Determine the kind of man you want to be and begin your journey towards becoming him. Step 3: Improve your wife's life by demonstrating that man to her.

This stuff works; it's not a gimmick or anything from me. It's just basic logic. I'm just a man who has witnessed a lot of men experience divorce and is passionate about assisting men like you in realizing the full potential they can have in their marriage. I've seen that this tactic helps most men keep their marriages intact, and I think it can do the same for you.

The most frequent ways I've witnessed men unintentionally push their wives away during separation are covered in the following chapter, along with suggestions for getting her back.

The Primary Cause of Women Divorcing Their Husbands

Women are currently starting divorces as a trend. According to a recent study including over 2200 couples, women are more likely to file for divorce. In 69 percent of cases, this is in contrast to the 31 percent of divorces that men start. I spoke with relationship coach and therapist Rick Brown to elaborate on this.

This is the result of the fact that women in your parents' age are capable of earning their own money. When my parents were growing up, wives were usually the breadwinners and cared for the home. Women may now financially say, "I can leave this relationship if I'm not happy," because two people are employed.

It is a little bit easier for me to rely on myself.

Apart from the fact that time is changing, what do you think is the underlying cause of this trend? Do you believe that women's tolerance for bad relationships may be waning?

By the way, the majority of people who are thinking about women are also considering divorce. Their true desire is to put an end to their suffering, which for many women is the feeling of being alone or emotionally estranged from their partner. They don't want a divorce.

And there's a sense that says, "I want everything; I want to feel closer to my partner."

We discussed the general trajectory of a relationship, wherein you're filled with excitement, contentment, and an overwhelming sense of love when entering a new one. Correct? However, we are aware that partnerships evolve with time. Do you discover that individuals are unwilling to make the necessary investments in the connection to revive it?

They're not sure how to accomplish it, though. They don't know how to do it but want to. Therefore, men frequently experience the same feelings of emotional isolation or disconnection from women in marriages. They simply lack the words to express it. So, the lady who says, "I'm unhappy, I don't like this, and I'm feeling lonely at it," is frequently the one speaking. However, it frequently comes across as criticism, which makes people defensive and leads to arguments.

It's common to hear therapists lament, "Gosh, I wish couples would come to me sooner," because, by the time they reach out to them to attempt to see if they can work things out, it's generally too late. You'll be more successful when you catch it upstream instead of downstream. However, I get excited when people come in, no matter what time of day.

They are essentially asking things like, "I'm stuck, I need help, I'm in pain, can you help us get," and I believe that the true goal of these requests is to reconnect and become more connected. The bulk of users on Ashley Madison's website were men, as one of the things we saw. Do you think that the males may be saying to themselves, "You know what, I'll just do my little thing on the side to keep me happy, but I want to stay," as a reason they may not want to end the relationship?

Indeed, men tend to find comfort in stability at home, which affairs typically provide. They assist in maintaining the relationship by making returning home slightly more tolerable when something is happening over here rather than between us. And most of the time, they manage to keep a relationship stable. Naturally, the relationship is destroyed as soon as it is detected or found out.

GETTING THE BEST EVER HAPPY AFTER BADGE

If you've successfully got your ex back, be sure you're not hiding who you truly are. Individuals might learn small tricks to trick others into talking or acting a certain way to keep them interested.

This is a worrying way to behave because it's not who you are. If you're not being real, who's falling for you? And what will they think of the real you once you pull the plug and start being yourself again?

If you're serious about reconnecting with your ex, resist the urge to employ mind tricks, manipulation, or other foolish tactics to get others to love you. Simply be yourself.

You may still envision the confident, cheerful, and merry person they both find appealing.

It can be hard to accept the end of a relationship, especially if you are in love with your ex.

But if you have the tolerance, understanding, and flexibility to adapt, you can try to get your ex back.

▫ Give yourself some time.

Allowing oneself space and time to heal after a breakup is important. Giving your ex a break means doing things like unfollowing them on social media or not communicating with them at all.

During this time, focus on your wants and needs alone rather than trying to get your ex back.

Reflecting on the past helps you identify what went wrong in the relationship and what you could have done differently.

Admit your failings and mistakes ruthlessly, and consider how you might grow as a partner.

⬛ Have candid and open communication

You must be upfront and sincere about your feelings and goals to regain your ex's affection.

This is listening to their point of view and trying to understand it even if it's difficult.

It's also critical to be willing to make adjustments, change the relationship, and be honest and upfront with yourself about your wants and goals.

[6] If you want to regain your former's affection, demonstrate to them that you have changed. You must demonstrate to your former partner that you have grown as a spouse. This could be

regarded as being more considerate, understanding, or willing to compromise. It could also mean showing your former partner you are dedicated to settling outstanding issues.

It's not going to happen overnight, so be patient. It will require time, patience, and effort to rebuild trust and show your ex that you are committed to making things work. If things take a while, try not to lose hope and be nice and patient.

▢ Seek assistance

Talking to friends, relatives, or a therapist about your feelings and desire to get your ex back can be helpful.

If you have done everything and your ex isn't interested in trying again, it might be time to accept that the relationship is over and move on.

Letting go of the past can be challenging when trying to move forward.

It's important to remember that getting your ex back won't be easy and might not even be possible. However, being honest, open, and willing to make changes may increase the likelihood that the relationship will get better.

It might be worth it if you genuinely love your ex and have a brighter future together.

◆ Show your former partner your progress.

If you want your ex to fall in love with you again after the breakup, you must show them how much you've grown.

This could be striving to improve yourself, like taking up new hobbies or interests or emphasizing personal growth.

By proving to your ex that you have changed and are committed to bettering yourself, you can show them that you are ready for a fresh start in a new and better relationship.

Although it could be tempting to woo your ex with extravagant gifts or showy gestures, these actions usually drive a wedge between you. Instead, emphasize true, authentic discussion and connection.

It's important to take things gently since you shouldn't start a new relationship before you and your ex are ready. Hastily proceeding may lead to miscommunications and conflicts, impeding your attempts to regain your former partner's affection.

Adopt a positive outlook.
If you want to make your ex fall in love with you again, you must think

positively about your relationship and the things that initially pulled you together.

Recall the enjoyable moments and pursuits you engaged in together and try to replicate them.

Above all, when trying to win back your ex-lover, it's important to be true and honest. Rather than trying to con or control your former partner, be open and truthful about your intentions.

Being genuine and transparent will show your ex that you are committed to fixing the relationship and making it work.

Be the best version of yourself that you can be. Keep a positive attitude, look for the good in everything, and figure out how to be happy.

Enjoy your friends and your hobbies or interests.

You can project confidence when you look and feel your best.

Your ex loved you for who you were when you first met at the end of the day.

He or she will most likely stay in love with you just as you are. So that they can fall in love with you again, give him/her your best self.

Chapter 3: Primary Causes of Couples' Dissolution

"A real man in a relationship makes other people jealous of his woman, not the other way around."
Maraboli Steve

I'll talk to you about the primary causes of couple breakups in this book section. The best way to handle this situation is to determine the causes behind the relationship breakdown. Being completely aware of why most relationships fail can also benefit you and enable you to take steps to ensure that the same problems don't arise in the future or negatively impact you in new relationships.

Here are some common causes of couple breakups, some of which you may be able to identify with:

There's Someone Who's Cheating

Naturally, choosing to see someone else in a committed relationship is a major factor in the breakdown of many wonderful partnerships. Very few people desire to remain in the company of an unfaithful lover. Regaining trust and stability to proceed is quite tough when you discover that someone else is participating in a relationship. Cheating damages trust, which is the foundation of all successful relationships.

It's quite difficult to rebuild trust and repair a relationship if cheating issues cause your relationship to dissolve. However, it is more difficult; it is still achievable.

Someone Has Negative Behaviour

After spending a great deal of time together, you clearly understand your partner's genuine nature. Their patterns become much more apparent. These days, some couples break down because one partner has unpleasant, negative, and problematic qualities. These could include the following:

Having an uncontrollably messy appearance, having a short fuse, lying excessively, having an uncontrollably high blood alcohol content, having a drug problem, and even forgetting to say "I love you."

There's a chance your lover will leave you and find someone else if they discover these qualities in you and find them unappealing. Individuals with unmanageable bad habits are not people anyone wants to be around. Because they want to ensure their partner has no uncontrollable habits, folks wait long before proposing.

I want you to consider if your negative habits are why the relationship ended. If so, you will have a much better chance of gaining your ex back and keeping them if you can learn how to quit the habit and/or replace it with a much healthier one.

AN APPROPRIATE AMOUNT OF ORGANISATION AND IMPACT

One of the most important components of a successful partnership is communication. But it's also a major factor in the breakup of successful partnerships. It will come off as annoying if you bombard your girlfriend with excessive amounts of text messages, phone calls, and affection. Your lover will naturally leave you if you show them too little affection and communication since they will think you don't love them.

Both excessive and insufficient communication are undesirable. It needs to remain in balance.

Money Issues

I'm not suggesting that your partner is in your life just because of your wealth. However, persistent arguments over money lead to many marriage dissolutions. These could include any of the following:

- Spending that isn't essential; debt; gambling

Many of these charges may arise if your ex's breakup was due to financial difficulties. To reconcile with your partner, you must take care of any outstanding debt and ensure it doesn't arise again once you get your ex back.

Abuse, either verbal or physical

Any physical violence is a red flag that your relationship is toxic, and you should end it. But even disparate types of abuse, like verbal and emotional abuse, might cause someone to want to break up with someone. Relationships should be built on mutual love and respect, not based on hurting the other person. Abuse of any kind is never acceptable.

For the benefit of both your well-being and your partner's, you should carefully consider whether you want to return to your relationship if it is terminated due to abuse of any kind. The best course of action is to end a relationship if it is unsafe.

Partner's Value System Is Different

Values are opinions on what you consider proper and inappropriate, right and wrong. They remain constant in our thoughts and influence who we are now.

Our parents, teachers, religious authorities, and other significant and strong individuals instill our values in us early on. Values serve as the foundation for our personal growth. Since values help us respect ourselves and others, it's possible that your spouse doesn't share your values or is very different from yours, which could lead to a breakup.

Relationships with persons who share similar interests and characteristics are desirable to many people. You can overcome whatever obstacle life throws at you if you find someone with whom you click well. There will be a great deal of tension if one spouse holds certain values and the other does not, which could lead to the two of you splitting up quickly.

Absence of Interest

Whatever the cause of your ex's breakup, it was probably due to a decline in interest. They just didn't want to spend any more time with you. All relationships now terminate due to a loss of attractiveness, which can be brought on by unattractive personalities, poor habits, or tiredness of being around you. Now that you know your ex isn't attracted to you, you need to figure out what changed your relationship for a split. After that, there's the beginning portion. To get your ex to come crawling back to you, you must figure out how to spark this reattraction in them. Knowing your ex and what they seek in a partner should simplify this. Simply recreate that character.

Naturally, there are a plethora of diverse reasons why partnerships fail. However, you must ensure that, if any of the causes above apply to you, you address them immediately. If you continue to harbor grudges about why you two broke up, your partner will not want to get back together. The best course of action is to identify and solve the problem.

Recognizing The Significance Of A Divorce Or Split

Experiencing a painful breakup might make it difficult to see that there are opportunities to grow and learn. Things can and will change, even though all you feel right now is emptiness and despair. Consider this time in your life as a break and an opportunity to sow the seeds of fresh development. After this interaction, you might feel stronger, wiser, and have a clearer sense of who you are.

To effectively accept a breakup and move on, you must understand what happened and accept your role. You'll understand how your choices affected the relationship more fully and more.

Considerations For Your Questions

Look at the bigger picture from a distance. What role did you play in the problems in the relationship?

Do you consistently choose the wrong partners for relationships or commit the same mistakes?

Think about the ways you manage stress, conflict, and insecurities. Could you act more constructively?

Consider your ability to accept others for who they are rather than for what you believe they "should" or "could" be.

To bring about change, start by analyzing your negative feelings. Do your feelings dominate you, or do you have control over them?

You have to be real with yourself during this healing time. Refrain from assigning blame or berating yourself for your mistakes. As you reflect on the relationship, you can learn more about who you are, how you interact with people, and the problems you still need to fix. If you can look objectively at your actions and decisions, including the reasons behind your choice of an ex-partner, you will be able to recognize your mistakes and steer clear of them going forward.

Let's get started, sweetheart.

MANAGEMENT TIPS FOR OVERCOMING A CRUSH OR LOST RELATIONSHIP

Maybe you caught him cheating on you, and you two had a happy ever after. It's possible that she moved away, and you two had a wonderful relationship that had to stop. Perhaps you were rejected by the mysterious girl in your gym class who kept glancing at you, or perhaps the guy you thought would improve your life didn't want you. There's a reason you're here, and it's because you lost someone. As you read this, there is only one person on your mind. You feel uncomfortable and depressed since you know that this person shouldn't be on your mind. After reading this essay, you should be better able to move past your disastrous crush or failed romance and be stronger for the next difficult few days.

Acknowledge that you are not alone. Though moving past rejections and breakups can be extremely challenging, remember that hundreds of others have been in your position. Not everyone has the same feelings as you. But know that you will triumph over this and become stronger.

Give your body time to heal. Realize that you can't expect yourself to let go right away because the hurt was just sustained. Give yourself a few days to think, cry, contemplate, and wonder. If you desire a successful recovery, you must allow yourself to go through the grieving process. The pain can be lessened by expressing your emotions and crying. Put your trust in a trustworthy person and allow yourself to enjoy. It's possible to decompress in many ways besides hanging out with friends, eating well, watching movies or music, and engaging in hobbies. Before you begin to move on, you must give the person time to process the situation and find closure.

Delete the history. Once you've passed the early going, it's time to move on from your ex or ex-crush. You must move on from the person who hurt you even though you may be flooded with emotion. Regardless of your feelings, delete the texts, toss away the photos, and take them down from your social media profiles. If they give you gifts, save them in a box if you need them later. Avoiding triggers that may evoke unpleasant memories will help you learn to let go of a relationship that isn't meant to endure. There's no point in holding onto bad recollections.

Imagine traveling back in time. Within reason, consider your strained relationship as often as you'd like. Consider everything that went into the breakup and why the crush was short-lived. There was one, if not more than one, good cause, even though it might not have appeared to have one. Acknowledge that you used to appreciate each other, or at least the concept of each other. If it hadn't been what your partner wanted for the rest of their life, the relationship would have ended sooner or later, even though it seemed OK to you. Realize that it ended sooner rather than later for the best.

Write down every feeling you have. Make them poems or present them with a journal. There must be no self-editing and complete truthfulness. One of the best things about writing everything down is that sometimes you'll be astounded by a flash of insight when you're pouring your ideas onto paper. Perhaps more distinct patterns will show up. When your grief begins to fade, you'll find it easier to extract valuable life lessons from the whole experience if you've been journaling your way through it. No relationship or crush is ever a failure if you can keep your heart open to both joy and pain and use what you've been through to learn something about yourself. Something doesn't have to work out for you to be important to your growth into the person you were meant to be. Let learning, at the absolute least, make your life better.

Participate actively. Start focusing your attention elsewhere in life. Take up painting, working out, or starting a group. It's unnecessary to conclude that you're over or lost just because a relationship ended or things didn't go as planned.

Take pride in your identity. Enumerate all the good things about you and your life. Think of them as blessings. Love for oneself is sometimes the only thing that may make you feel better about yourself. If you think they broke up with you because you weren't their type or you weren't as attractive as the person they are currently dating, don't be too hard on yourself. The loser lost you, not the other way around, so it's time to get outside, work out, go to the spa, and take care of your looks. Realize that you are the winner.

Find a place to plug in. Maybe writing, music, or the presence of friends provideyou comfort. Give it some of your attention, whatever it may be. You could discover more about who you are than you already knew.

Try a new concept. Take up a new hobby, sport, or appearance.

Retain your dignity. Our ego frequently causes agony; we feel deceived, rejected, and ashamed. We doubt our value and adequacy. Breaking up can seriously impair your confidence and self-esteem, particularly if your partner cheated on you. For example, giving yourself something to be proud of—volunteering or taking a class—can help your inner equilibrium return.

Make new friends. But who knows? They might be the ones you have been searching for.

Avoid wallowing in your misery for too long. If not, you'll begin to lose friends and experience poor self-esteem. It's going to be difficult for you to overcome your predominant feeling of depression. It's critical to remember that you will unavoidably have this minor setback again in the future, so you need to get ready to handle it better the first time. Instead of thinking, "My life stinks because...." try saying, "My life is amazing because..." to help you concentrate on all the good things in your life rather than the awful things that have happened.

Turn on some music. You may identify with your struggles and use music to help you get over them. Listening to your MP3 player or iPod is crucial for the first several months. Even if it is just calming tunes. There is proof that music has calming effects on the psyche.

Chapter 8: Errors You Must Steer Clear Of At All Costs

It's not only about what you should do, even as we assist you in figuring out how to reconcile with your ex. You should avoid performing certain things since they will never be able to mend your relationship. After reading through people's common blunders, you will see why it matters.

Error 1: Constantly phoning or messaging the former partner

Most people tend to overreact and keep contacting others via text or phone. Usually, it's a frantic and instinctual attempt to establish a connection with the other person, hoping it could be helpful.

In actuality, though, it is the opposite. This type of behavior presents a needy, desperate, and unattractive picture. It can even exacerbate the situation.

You may believe things will get worse if you don't give them a call. However, there's a better way to deal with this than just constantly blowing up their phone.

Some people give in to their impulse to pick up the phone when they are intoxicated, even if they can resist it otherwise. Therefore, put your phone out of reach or stay with a friend who won't allow you to make such blunders if you decide to use alcohol as a strategy to cope with your sadness.

Error 2: Pleading

Is it appropriate to beg for someone's attention? Ask yourself this question carefully. It doesn't just work; it also gives you a helpless, desperate expression. And you most certainly don't want that.

Should that be your reconciliation method, the other person will see through your weakness and continue manipulating your emotions. Ensure you act in a way that will support your continued relationship if you manage to get your ex back this time.

It's not about proving to them that you depend on them and will stop at nothing to reunite. It is not appropriate for you to reconcile out of sympathy.

To get back together, you have to do things that show them how much they love and respect you. Don't go begging, please.

Error 3: Behaving like a doormat

You may feel that doing whatever they ask of you will help, and you may want to get back together with them at all costs.

But that is not going to help at all. Making the other person happy to grant their requests is not the goal.

To keep someone with you, you shouldn't have to act like a doormat and give up everything. Whatever the circumstances, letting someone walk all over you is absurd and harmful.

We'll say it again: respect is crucial to a relationship. Your needs and wants will be entirely ignored if they are led to believe that only theirs matters. In a relationship like that, would you be content?

Error 4: Seeking too much assistance from others

You should rely on friends and family for support, but you shouldn't use them to get back together with your ex.

You might believe that if your ex speaks with one of them, they'll understand how much you value them and that it's time for you two to get back together.

First, there are situations in which the person you trust can actively work against you to exacerbate the situation. The possibility of the broth spoiling due to an excessive number of cookers is another drawback in this situation.

Your relationship is truly only understood by you and your ex, so while you sort things out, it should be between you. They would find it annoying if others tried interfering with their lives.

Error 5: Just pals

You are mistaken if you believe that telling the other person that all you want is to be friends will be successful. They will entirely remove you from any romantic ideas they may have if you do this. All you'll get out of this is "friend zoned."

You should be truthful with the other person and yourself if you desire a connection beyond friendship. Don't act one way and talk another.

Building a friendly relationship is a positive move, but there's a difference between being nice and being friend-zoned.

Your friendship should serve as a foundation for your partnership by improving your understanding of one another. You don't want them to approach you and start gushing about another lovely person.

Thus, use caution when using your friend card.

Error 6: Using their backup plan

This is common if your ex ended things and started dating someone else.

They might come back to you as a backup plan if turned down. When you are very accessible, people start to take advantage of you.

Nobody should make you their backup plan. Long-term success is contingent upon your status as their backup plan.

Don't return to them because you wanted them more than everyone else did. This is not necessary.

Error 7: Companions with advantages

Don't give your ex the impression that they can get away with hurting you because of your feelings when you're trying to get back together.

Do not be their booty call, even though it is entirely up to you to have close contact with them even after the breakup.

If you still get together and accept full responsibility for your behavior, that's

OK. Sex is not the means to return someone's favor. as that isn't how it will operate.

Intimacy is vital, but it wasn't the reason you broke up, was it? You must address what went wrong the first time to make it last the second time.

Error 8: Calming your pride

Some of you genuinely love your ex and want to be with them again, but others have different goals.

As you proceed, ask yourself honestly. Do you desire their return? Or perhaps you simply can't take rejection well?

It's not appropriate to pursue someone to boost your ego. You don't have to be concerned about falling short of someone. If things do not work out, there are several possible explanations. Someone else will want you even if they no longer do. It's not the end of the world to be rejected.

Error 9: Becoming overly possessive if they go out with someone else

It doesn't matter whether your ex is dating someone else. Do you believe that is a big deal for them, especially shortly after the breakup? They most likely jumped in as a way to recover.

First, don't strive to win them back merely out of possessiveness. You should only consider getting back together with your ex if you genuinely want them back in your life, not because you have a possession mentality.

Don't act childish and sabotage their brand-new partnership. You don't have to feel like you must outdo everyone else to be in his life.

You will be together if it is your destiny. Don't undermine the new person in his life; work to make him understand your importance.

Error 10: Purchasing their affection

Although men typically use this strategy, women can also use it to get their exes back. Buying them cards and gifts is inappropriate to make them feel special. Instead, you can come out as excessively desperate or as someone pretending to be honest about their feelings and trying to buy them back.

Presents cannot make up for the shortcomings in your partnership.

Thus, before making such deliveries, give it some thought. You can't buy love for yourself.

These are only a few fundamentals; although some of you may think they go without saying, you are unaware of your blunders until they happen. So before you go out on your campaign to win your ex back, remember these. Otherwise, it might potentially work against you.

PERSERVANCE AS A VIRTUE

When you hurt and truly want your ex back, it might be hard to wait patiently. Your chances of getting your ex to confess they still love you will decrease if you rush things. The window of opportunity to win your ex back is endless. Due to various circumstances, each situation is unique, and timing and getting over your ex are crucial. The more you press the issue, the quicker you confirm that you haven't changed and aren't prepared to put in the effort necessary to mend your relationship. You'll come across as shallow and surface-level.

Nothing ever returns to as it was. Once anything is spoken, it cannot be taken back. When you can both admit to each other that you acted out of grief and anger and are sorry for what you said, that's when the healing starts. You must demonstrate this by doing something overt, like enrolling in a relationship class—even by yourself. You will have to demonstrate your sincere desire to change to show it. Even if your ex insists there's no way you'll ever get back, you still need to prove you understand and are mistaken. If you truly do change, there's always a chance.

This kind of change won't happen instantly; in certain situations—like

Greg's case—it might never happen. In other cases, your ex might not be able to forgive you at all. This can occasionally mean that true patience is tested and developed into a virtue for the next relationship. You have to get ready for such an eventuality. However, you will be happier if you do not give up and keep improving yourself. You'll be happy that you handled yourself responsibly in retrospect, and perhaps your former partner will, too.

Embracing Adaptation

Human nature dictates that we like things to remain as they are. At least you are aware of the situation you find yourself in, but that is not how life works, and change is a given. Without a doubt, relationships evolve throughout time. The goal is to continuously improve each other's value. You can grow in a way that respects one another if you acquire the abilities required to deal with change.

Recognizing that things have changed includes accepting that your ex needs distance, might not want a reconciliation, or could require more time than you would like to offer them. You must change your behavior should you and your ex decide to get back together.

Recall that separations can be a healthy approach for partners to decompress and work through their issues while giving each other space.

Right now, you and your ex are both hurting. You both understand that you need to transform on the inside. Make changes because they are healthy for you, not only to get your ex back. What reveals your actual nature is how you behave under pressure. This character can either bring your ex back to you or drive them away completely.

Chapter 7: The Comeback

You might be ready for reconciliation after an emotionally taxing thirty days of being secretive, refusing to communicate in any way, and having to thwart any attempts to show your desperation.

However, there are still a few things you should think about. For example, you have no way of knowing if your former partner has faced the same difficulties that you have. You're not entirely certain if they'll be open to making amends. Furthermore, you're not sure that 30 days is sufficient for feelings to subside.

More assumptions are just going to feed presumptions. The problem is that assuming your ex still has concerns, the

30-day term plus your exclusion should be enough to get their attention.

Nevertheless, it is wise to take a chance once the emotions have subsided. It could be a good idea to have a little conversation now that your tension has already subsided.

Request

Even briefly, you could start a conversation with a short text or private message.

First, though, think about the time. Since you both have the weekend free from work and would be up for a conversation, sending your ex a casual "Hello" message might be a good idea.

You are free to send now that you have the advantage of time. The moment you press the transmit button is critical. There can be a reason why your ex would either respond to you or ignore you. Eventually, he or she might reply to you with something, perhaps even just a casual "Hello" with a smile.

This is your opportunity to continue the discussion. Inquire about your ex's well-being, but avoid bringing up the breakup. Be as informal as possible while attempting to steer the conversation toward a potential reunion.

Concerning a Reunion

During your talk, specifics of the breakup can come up. Even so, it's preferable if your ex made the request. You've been "underground" long enough for him or her to be interested in how you're following the breakup. They want to know how you are addressing the void.

Be truthful in your response. Tell your ex how different your life is without them, straight from the heart. Most likely, your former partner may have gone through a similar experience of feeling empty and is equally eager to make things work once more.

Get Together

Try to be mindful of one another's emotions when you converse about the relationship. Never take charge of the conversation and let your ego run wild. Both of you will have an overwhelming sense of nostalgia in this way. You'll start to rediscover one another and feel the same closeness that formerly ruled your relationship.

If everything goes too smoothly, get together at a location with special meaning for you, and then you can start over.

Embrace Your Body's Flirt

If you both feel comfortable with each other, move forward and approach her. Your body language should convey that you desire to get close to her.

Flirting is more than just talking. Rather, how you handle your body language and let it do the talking could be a big turn-on for a woman.

Liz has said I have excellent body language and seem to improve daily. I put my arm around her shoulder and let her lean on me as we shared our first kiss.

After that, I rubbed her cheek and tucked a hair behind her ear. She was in love.

These tiny gestures will make her feel more comfortable when you touch her.
Establish the Perfect Setting

Now that she seems comfortable with you, it's time to become serious. Creating the perfect setting is the first move in luring her in. She can listen to some music to lift her spirits.

Make sure you also know what kind of music she likes. Experts suggest playing soft music to evoke a sexual atmosphere. It could be a great place to start when getting a woman.

I'll play some of her favorite songs when we have some alone time together.
Remember that she is the center of attention, not you. Thus, keep her from

getting bored and play the music you know she'll enjoy.

The environment has a big impact on seduction as well. Consider adding some candles and fresh rose petals to spruce up the area a bit.

Make Physical Contact

Now is the time to initiate physical contact, but proceed with caution. Imagine the two of you strolling in a park or beside a lake. Gently massage her back and take her hand to lead her around the path. Claim to be leading her.

One way you can intervene is by:

Approaching her and making contact with her knee or back. Don't go too fast, or else she might take your hands off her body.

Keeping it gentle and flowing. Despite the length of time we had known one another, I never attempted to appear desperate during any sexual encounter.

The secret to wooing a woman is surprisingly easy: keep things simple, move deliberately, and refrain from going too rapidly. The right tempo keeps the flow flowing; going too quickly or violently can be unsettling.

I blew her my first kiss, a warm, passionate one. If this is your first time touching her, observe how she kisses to understand her preferences.

If you've been dating for a while, you can try to break the pattern by trying a new profession or place! Have a great evening together, choose the kitchen, or even shower together.

Chapter 2: The Operation of the No Contact Rule

It's time to flip the script and have your ex come after you. You must reclaim all authority and control. You probably think that, at this point, your ex is the only one who can determine whether or not you two get back together, but that isn't true at all. Sounds too good to be true, doesn't it? Listen to me.

Whatever the circumstances between you and your ex are, I'm sure you're not happy about it, and I'm going to assume that you're the one who ended things. When they terminate things, the person who dumps, or the "dumper," is typically in a powerful position. The individual being broken up with, or the dumpee, has little power.

They know that when you were dumped, you most likely thought you would stop at nothing to win your ex back.

You must take away their safety net and turn the tables on them. Allow us to push them beyond their comfort zone. They will be the ones who do this.

Begin to pursue you. Showing them that you no longer need them would be a wonderful place to start. How would one go about doing this? You will not speak with them for thirty days. They will be completely taken aback by this coming from you. Your former partner still feels as though they have you completely under control. They believe that all they need to do is make a simple request, and you will quickly return. But when you break off all communication with them, that's not the message they will hear.

By ceasing all communication, you are letting someone know that you are, at least in part, prepared to move on and start a new relationship. They have no idea that it might not be true.

They'll go nuts and start thinking about you all the time if weeks go by and they still haven't heard from you. They will begin to doubt themselves and wonder if it was a poor idea to end things with you in the first place.

Ever ponder why former partners attempt to maintain friendships? They see it as a backup plan. They regret splitting up with you or going back to their previous behavior. Or if the opposite side's grass isn't greener. However, leaving them with no trace indicates that you will disappear and that they must decide now if they want you in their lives. By the way, you should never consider becoming friends. Nobody should use you as a backup plan. No one's backup plan is you. You are more valuable than that!

The comfort zone is what the unconscious mind longs for. It hurts them to be apart from you, even if they started the split. You can't give in, even if your ex calls you again. It is not your intention to provide emotional assistance. They must realize that they must decide whether to pursue a relationship with you. You wish to keep your feelings to yourself if you believe it is not possible—for instance, if you cohabitate or have a kid together. Avoid projecting insecurity. Act content should not be exposed. Go out frequently. Avoid staying at home. Even though they might start dating someone else, you want to appear indifferent. If you persevere, your ex will eventually open up to you, and things will turn around. Don't give up; the no-touch method is effective in virtually all situations.

Chapter 3: Will My Former Partner Ignore Me?

Not only do many people believe they have valid reasons for attempting to get in touch with their former partner, but this couldn't be further from the reality. You should stay away from them.

You will be well on your way to learning how to apply the no-contact rule if you can always keep your mouth shut around them.

You wish to introduce them to life without you. All of their bad recollections of you and the reasons the relationship ended in the first place will begin to fade. All of your relationship's happier moments will begin to come back to you.

When those memories have peaked, they will be more receptive and willing to talk to you. However, I know your fear—that they will forget about you.

Will they, however, forget me? You scream.

NO is the response. Your ex will never, ever forget about you. You possess memories, inside jokes, routines, history, and other things that have grown over months and years.

The memories they have of you will only be strengthened by this distance. (However, you must provide them with new, positive perceptions of you instead of the negative ones they currently have). You want to think of yourself as a better, updated version.

Don't worry, though; the prohibition of communication will make them miss you more! The strong feelings, such anguish, and heartbreak, will subside, and the initial reasons for their love will come back to you.

WHEN A FAVORABLE RELATIONSHIP GOES WELL

Unfortunately, even the strongest relationships can fall from time to time. However, there's always a reason for it, even if we don't recognize it at first.

To be honest, there are many reasons why happy marriages fall apart and result in divorce. You might have had to endure meaningless disagreements or just learned that your former partner abruptly stopped communicating with you before withdrawing and keeping you in the dark. When someone is hurting and unclear of their spouse's role in the relationship, they often do the opposite of what is recommended to get their former partner back.

This is so that men don't always follow what makes sense to a male, and women don't try strategies they wouldn't like to see. One important lesson to learn is that men and women think differently. Generally speaking, attempting to win back a female is as futile as attempting to win back a male using female logic.

The truly unfortunate part of this is that try, as they might, both men and women in these situations tend to mistakenly act in ways that alienate and push away the very person they are trying so hard to get back.

This indicates that often, without even realizing it, they're doing the exact opposite of what they ought to be doing to win their ex back and reintegrate them into their lives. Think about things for a while. Are your current attempts to get your ex back going well? Or does it just make you feel farther apart from that other, intensifying your unfavorable emotions?

We can better understand these viewpoints by looking at some of the factors that men and women take into account in relationships and how they interpret their partner's actions. These "lightbulb moments" can often result in a far better grasp of what could have gone wrong in the relationship and a deeper comprehension of what to do when healthy relationships falter.

The biology of men and women differs.

Although this may seem like a statement of the obvious, there are important hormonal and other biological distinctions that distinguish us in addition to the evident differences.

For instance, did you know that men frequently look for ways to enhance testosterone to reduce their levels of stress? This suggests that following a demanding workday, people will watch the news to devise fixes and go into "fix it" mode on their own. This implies that they can take pleasure in tackling the issues of others since it makes them feel compelled to attempt to resolve global issues.

Even though he appears to be sitting passively on the sofa, he might be thinking about that. He will not be able to assist with problems in the actual world until he controls his stress levels. When their testosterone levels are higher, they will feel a lot better about the world and wait to try solving their issues until they have had enough time to cool off after a demanding workday in which they have tried to be a good provider.

Sadly, women's biological drives differ greatly from men's, which can cause problems in relationships. For example, a woman with higher testosterone levels in her body may be more anxious and prone to argue with her boyfriend about trivial matters that she knows he won't understand.

Women will develop ways to produce the hormone oxytocin to lower their stress levels. Oddly, oxytocin is called the "cuddle hormone" in non-scientific circles and has been closely associated with maternal behavior. It is also the hormone that promotes stronger bonds between partners and women.

Now, women must experience love, adoration, and appreciation for them to produce oxytocin. Instead, the hormone testosterone floods their system, increasing stress levels and sometimes making them defensive when they feel that their partner is pulling away from them for any reason.

On the other hand, when a man's testosterone levels drop, he also has a comparable reaction that causes him to become more protective due to an increase in stress. Interesting content

How Hormones Can Spoil a Perfect Relationship

Think back to the occasions when you were happy and excited to see your lover.

You would have been involved in activities that boosted your confidence throughout the day. If you're a woman, you may have spent some time discussing various issues with your girlfriends to decompress, raising your oxytocin levels.

It would have felt amazing!

But when your ex got home from work after a long day, he was probably anxious and nervous. He doesn't want to talk about his problems because talking about them makes the wrong hormone surge in his body. All he wants to do is relax, and maybe the world's problems can be fixed while he watches TV for a short while.

But now that he is experiencing significant and potentially even uncontrollable levels of stress, he must deal with a spouse who longs for affection, communication, sharing, and cuddles. He's hardly had time to recover from his demanding day, and now he has to cope with a partner who doesn't seem to care about him or comprehend what he wants. Even though this is a simple example, can you spot the problem? Even the best relationships might fail if there is a lack of knowledge about these fundamental hormonal variations between men and women.

Of course, there are additional causes for failed partnerships.

Relationships that fall apart for different reasons

What occurs if you abide by every guideline, yet your former partner keeps putting distance between you?

Sometimes, relationships end with no apparent explanation at all. Your ex may have decided to cease communicating with you by phone or text and to end the relationship completely as if you never existed, even though you may have felt that everything was going well.

The person who has fully withdrawn may have very different beliefs about how the relationship was originally headed. Still, the person who has been ignored often feels they have done nothing wrong.

The hormones released by people who fall in love are, in fact, extremely similar to those released by persons who suffer from OCD (OCD). This is one of the reasons why people in love find it difficult to eat, sleep peacefully, concentrate at work, or think about anything but the person they are with.

Of course, this does not imply that your spouse felt the same thing at the same moment as you. Just like not everyone gets hungry simultaneously, not everyone feels the same feelings simultaneously. The bad thing about this is that now and then, one of the people involved in the relationship may begin to think about taking it further. They will take some time to think through potential outcomes and envision different situations for when the relationship progresses beyond the dating phase.

Because of this, one person may believe that the relationship has progressed beyond its true state, while the other person may simply be trying to make sense of their feelings. Another name for this is an "instant relationship." One party believes they are merely dating, while the other is in full relationship mode and questioning why their partner doesn't appear to reciprocate.

Trying to convince their partner that they should be together or that they are madly in love with them is the biggest mistake anyone can make in this situation. When males witness women behaving this way, they may feel compelled to slow down or perhaps go, as they are left wondering what is happening.

They may withdraw entirely or isolate themselves because they believe their spouse is desperate and needy. An insecure and desperate lady turns men off completely.

But many guys are guilty of giving the women they love the same treatment. They could try to convince her that he is a better choice for her because he loves her more than any other man. These are challenging situations since it's hard for them to understand that they're doing things wrong.

ENTERTAINING THEM BACK INTO YOUR LIFE

The ability to win people over and draw them to you is called charm. It's not about manipulating others with power plays, drama, stress, or suffering. Don't mix trying to control someone with trying to charm them to win your ex back. Playing games with your ex is the best way to ensure they never want you back.

You will need to be cordial and take things easy. You must act like you don't mind if they start dating someone else. They will only become more distant from you and closer to someone else if you become nasty and ask them questions.

A friendship can be restored by talking about the good times and laughing with your ex in a secure and supportive environment. Anything is possible when you are friends again, but maintaining your friendship with your ex requires treating them like genuine friends and never going too far.

You must proceed cautiously. Remain composed and focus on your goals instead of allowing your feelings to rule you. Friendship must exist. To truly be trusted, you must never step over a line to manipulate your former partner, as doing so will defeat the purpose of true, rekindled love.

Be the person who captured their hearts.

How much did you evolve while you were dating your former partner? The honeymoon is over, and you can finally enjoy what you've always wanted. This is a really risky way of thinking. It won't take long for cracks to show if you weren't who you were when dating.

Many partnerships develop routines, and couples grow accustomed to one another. Habits take hold over time and might lead to issues in a relationship. How long until your ex starts moaning about you changing into someone else that you used to be in love with?

Did your fitness and self-care impact your ex's attraction to you? Did you get too serious if you were funny? Were you paying attention, acting kindly, and then ceasing to act kindly? You know your identity before the relationship and what drew your former partner to you.

Next, you should ask yourself whether you're content with the person you've become. How can your ex be pleased with you if the answer is no and you are unsatisfied with yourself? It's time to reflect on your goals and aspirations for the future and put those into practice.

Go ahead and be who you were before you and your ex started dating if that's what you want. You'll likely get much attention in the correct category and from more people than just your ex.

It will boost your confidence and encourage you to break free from the same routine. You'll also see the positive aspects of your former partner and stop wearing rose-colored glasses to view the world. You've already won half the war if you can concede that the reason your ex stopped loving you was because you changed.

You can decide not to wish to have the same kind of relationship with your ex if you have found your true self and are content with who you are.

Introducing Charles

Charles is an extremely kind man who went above and beyond for his partner. He believed that by giving her everything, he would win her affection even more. It didn't; his girlfriend decided she needed a real man and felt he was a wimp. She almost immediately started dating another man after breaking up with him. Charles didn't want another lady in his life; thus, it crushed his heart.

After some time, Charles realized that his girlfriend had been bullying him and that this wasn't who he truly was. He decided to resume his regular hiking and gym visits. He cherished the tranquility he experienced in the great outdoors. After agreeing with who he was, he started going out with pals. He had learned a very important lesson from his ex: never compromise your identity to appease someone else.

After getting his body and self-worth back in check, he called his former girlfriend to wish her well in their future and express his gratitude for their time together. She wanted to get together for coffee as soon as possible. He accepted, and she was astounded when she saw him enter the room.

Knowing he would never date another woman like her, he grinned contentedly. He was almost thankful that she had been so ungrateful and self-centered. She grew envious when she saw how other women were staring at him. She desired to reunite with her lover, whom she had split up with a few weeks prior.

When he said "no," she almost toppled over in her chair. He told her that although he wished her well, he realized they weren't meant to be together. He suggested they could keep in touch, but their relationship would be limited to friendship. He was prepared to wait for a genuinely nice girl to fall in love with him since he knew that a true relationship was just around the corner.

You know, you can decide you don't desire their attention even if you go back to being who you were to get their attention.

Chapter 1: Something went wrong for you

You will realize at this point that you still have feelings for your ex. Why do you think that? Do you get envious when you witness them having time with someone else? Or are you simply having insomniac evenings at 2 am? Or perhaps it's the loneliness that brings that individual to mind.

Breakups are typically difficult to deal with. You may have good reason to let go of the person and stop thinking about them if your partner cheated on you or if you had a major argument. However, it might be difficult to move on and move past a relationship where little conflicts and fights are the only reason for its termination. Usually, we don't see it right away, and by the time we do, it's too late.

We're never quite sure why our relationship ended, even if there wasn't a major cause. However, that is how we perceive it; insignificant issues that go unnoticed cause relationships to end. Here are a couple of these items.

1. Excessive standards

We begin to anticipate too much from our relationship when we love someone too much. We begin to lose sight of how every person uniquely expresses love and emotions. We have started the first step towards a major argument at this precise moment when we start to act selfishly. Not that you should accept anything less; just remember that nobody is flawless. Humans are not supermen. After viewing television dramas, films, and love stories, we conjure up our fantastical worlds. However, we must understand that we do not live in a fantasy world where romance blossoms out of nowhere and two people fall in love; rather, we are citizens of this real world.

It is in our nature as humans to constantly strive for excellence. However, it's time to grow up and acknowledge perfection as an unachievable ideal. All you can do is strengthen your relationship with your spouse to such an extent that no matter what challenges you experience, you two can overcome them, and no storm can ever cause you to separate.

Not a single partner can read people's minds. Talk it out with the other person instead of assuming they understand your thoughts or what you want them to say or do. Your thoughts will remain hidden from the other person unless you express them. It's untrue if you believe that your mate completes you. As a consistent partner who gives you the love and attention you need and deserve, he or she only adds to your happiness and plays a significant role in your life.

2. Making other comparisons with your partner

Wishing your lover had the traits of someone else is OK. But what if you've found yourself wishing your lover was just like them all the time? That indicates you are heading incorrectly if that is the case. People compare in a variety of ways. For example, some may base their comparison on your beauty, profession, dress style, demeanor, or even how you treat and care for your spouse.

When you compare your partner to another person, it makes them feel bad about themselves and makes them question why you're not like them. They could also become envious. When you love someone too much and have intense feelings for them, it's acceptable to feel envious. Given that your partner is aware of your protective and possessive nature towards them, a small amount of jealousy is appropriate in a relationship. However, excessive jealousy can ruin a relationship.

3. Having problems with trust

Do you become curious when you are having a deep chat with your significant other, and suddenly, the phone beeps? Your partner immediately checks the phone and responds to the recent text message. The sender and subject of the message are not disclosed to you. If you had the chance, would you check his or her phone?

Someone is making a fool of themselves if they lie to you. The individual who deceives their partner into thinking they are telling the truth is unlucky. Why is that individual not lucky? That person is unfortunate since, in rare cases, a partner will love someone enough to guarantee they won't be betrayed.

For example, your significant other informed you that you would have dinner tonight. Knowing the location and time, you arrived early to avoid making your companion wait a long while for you. However, you discover that they haven't arrived after 20 minutes. Initially, how would you respond? You would undoubtedly lose your cool, become enraged, and assume that your partner had forgotten their agreement. You decide to stay for another fifteen to twenty minutes and then head out. You're so mad with them that you don't even consider whether they're OK. Based on your presumptive scenario, you simply conclude that the person you love doesn't care and isn't good enough for you. What takes place after that? They never give you a call and leave you with no message. You presume that your significant other made no effort to contact you. You haven't contacted them since your partner organized the event, extended the invitation, and ultimately failed to attend. After a few hours, you learn the truth and discover that your partner's absence was due to an accident. You should trust your partner and never make snap decisions because of this. Your companion will undoubtedly stick by you and love you through thick and thin if they have committed to you.

4. Having bothersome or negative behaviors

Are you unwilling to change your habits even when they annoy your partner? Do you ever bite your fingernails? Do you neglect to give your teeth a brush? Do you pluck your nose instead? Have you thought about the potential that your foul odor results from not using deodorant? Or do you just tune out everything that doesn't interest you and only pay attention to what interests you? Do you constantly find fault with everything the other person does? Is it your terrible habit to always bring up the past and make fun of your partner?

This has to end. It's normal to feel compelled to ridicule someone who repeatedly injures you and makes the same mistakes. However, it's crucial to your relationship that you give your spouse a sense of worth and acknowledge them for even the simplest actions. It is akin to your parents constantly warning you about something bad for you or constantly reminding you of your mistakes. You probably become angry and despise them for it. Your companion is in the same situation. Don't let them get to the point where they begin to despise or shun you.

5. A communication breakdown

Effective communication is crucial to ensure nothing is left unsaid when two individuals are together. The majority of unsaid emotions and unexpressed feelings might be very problematic. Think of yourself as a balloon that is gradually filling up with air and will finally explode at its maximum capacity. Emotions and sensations are no different. Everything builds up inside you until you finally explode and get incredibly messed up.

Every partnership has one person who dominates the other and typically believes that person to be better than the other. You have to understand that a partnership is about two individuals walking hand in hand—not one in front of the other, neither one behind—exactly together. In a disagreement, both parties must be willing to wait for the other to finish speaking before voicing their opinions. How do we proceed? The communication gap widens when we primarily say what we have to say, cut the other person off before they can say anything, or worse, fail to listen to them fully.

6. Constantly quarreling and fighting

We sometimes overlook the length of time we have been fighting with our spouse; that is when the majority of love is gone. We forget the other person's issues and instead focus on our interests and needs. We frequently become so self-centered that we fail to see the other person for who they truly are.

Accepting someone for who they are is necessary; trying to transform someone into someone else isn't love, as it seems you are altering them completely. Little disagreements should always be settled quickly; the more you avoid discussing them, the more heated the arguments become.

7. Time-related Problems

Many relationships conflict because one partner feels their spouse doesn't make time for them. This is a crucial element that every relationship has to take into account. Since they are constantly vying for your attention, you must give them time while you are close to them. Time has a significant impact. Spending time with someone helps you comprehend them better. When two individuals have a strong bond, they can overcome any obstacles. As an illustration, if one partner works, the other should attempt to modify their schedule to their needs and recognize that they also have a lot of outside obligations to attend to. As a result, the other person must ensure they are comfortable and have enough room to unwind. The working partner should also be aware that their partner has been waiting a long time for his or her love, care, and attention.

When two partners are employed, they typically have a good understanding of one another's challenges and concerns because their circumstances are similar. Despite this, both parties should set aside enough time to talk and devote the necessary amount of time to their relationship.

www.ingramcontent.com/pod-product-compliance
Lightning Source LLC
Chambersburg PA
CBHW052143110526
44591CB00012B/1833